Short Stories in English for Intermediate Learners:

Master English Reading, Vocabulary, and Grammar

Jackie Bolen

www.eslspeaking.org

Copyright © 2023 by Jackie Bolen

All rights reserved. No part of this publication may be reproduced, distributed, or transmitted in any form or by any means, including photocopying, recording or other electronic or mechanical means without the prior written permission of the publisher, except in the case of brief quotations in critical reviews and certain other non-commercial uses permitted by copyright law. For permission requests, write to the publisher/author at the following address: Jackie Bolen: jb.business.online@gmail.com.

Table of Contents

About the Author: Jackie Bolen...4
How to Use this Book..5
Online Dating...6
The Canucks Game..9
Who is That?..12
A Hiking Misadventure...15
A Trip to Europe..18
Max and Emily...21
The New Italian Restaurant 24
Ice Fishing in Manitoba...27
Getting Caught...30
Learning to Play Tennis...33
A Summer BBQ..36
The First Day of University...39
Making Homemade Pasta..42
The English Test...45
Applying for University 48
Beginner's Luck..51
Thanksgiving Dinner 54
Breaking Up..57
Christmas in May...60
Ghosted..63
Halloween...67
The Lost Wallet..70
Going Vegan...73
The Hangover...76
Getting a Part-Time Job..79
Before You Go..82

About the Author: Jackie Bolen

I taught English in South Korea for 10 years to every level and type of student. I've taught every age from kindergarten kids to adults. Most of my time has centered around teaching at two universities: five years at a science and engineering school in Cheonan, and four years at a major university in Busan where I taught upper-level classes for students majoring in English. In my spare time, you can usually find me outside surfing, biking, hiking, or snowshoeing. I now live in Vancouver, Canada.

In case you were wondering what my academic qualifications are, I hold a Master of Arts in Psychology. During my time in Korea, I completed both the Cambridge CELTA and DELTA certification programs. With the combination of almost ten years teaching ESL/EFL learners of all ages and levels, and the more formal teaching qualifications I've obtained, I have a solid foundation on which to offer advice to English learners.

I truly hope that you find this book useful. I would love it if you sent me an email with any questions or feedback that you might have.

ESL Speaking (www.eslspeaking.org)

YouTube: (www.youtube.com/c/jackiebolen)

Email: jb.business.online@gmail.com

You might also be interested in this book: Intermediate English Dialogues: Speak American English Like a Native Speaker with these Phrases, Idioms, & Expressions. It has hundreds of helpful English idioms and expressions. You can find it wherever you like to buy books. Learn to speak more fluently in American English.

How to Use this Book

This book is ideal for people who want to improve their reading comprehension skills and vocabulary. Or for people who are preparing to move to Canada and want to learn a little bit about the culture before doing that.

To get the most bang for your buck, I recommend doing the following:

- Read one story a day, instead of all the stories in a single day! The best readers are those who do it consistently each day.

- Be sure to do the questions for each story.

- Pay attention to the vocabulary words in **bold** (letters that are darker). Try to guess the meaning of the word, considering the other words in the sentence before looking it up in a dictionary. After that, write down any words that you don't know in a notebook to review later. Also consider making flashcards for these new words.

- Read the stories with a friend if possible. Discuss the questions together.

- If you're using this book to improve your TOEFL, TOEIC or IELTS reading scores, be sure to read the questions first so you can scan for the answers instead of reading every single word. After doing this, take more time to read the story in full.

Online Dating

Once upon a time, in a small town called Willowbrook, there lived a young woman named Emma. Emma was a kind-hearted and adventurous soul who had always dreamed of finding true love. However, living in a **close-knit** community made it challenging for her to meet new people.

Determined to change her fate, Emma decided to try her luck with online dating. Her friends have always encouraged her to sign up, but she was reluctant. Now was the time though!

With her laptop in hand, Emma signed up for a popular dating website called "LoveConnect." She created an honest and **captivating** profile, highlighting her love for hiking, photography, and volunteering. Soon enough, she began receiving messages from various people who were intrigued by her interests.

Among the messages, there was one that stood out. It was from a man named Alex, who shared Emma's passion for the outdoors. His message was **genuine** and filled with enthusiasm. Intrigued, Emma decided to reply, sparking the beginning of their online journey.

Over the next few weeks, Emma and Alex exchanged messages daily. They discovered many similarities, such as their love for animals and their dreams of traveling the world. Their conversations gradually grew deeper, filled with shared dreams, fears, and aspirations. Emma felt a sense of comfort and trust in their connection, as if she had known Alex for a lifetime.

With their virtual relationship **blossoming**, Emma and Alex decided it was time to take the next step. They planned to meet face-to-face for the first time at a local café in Willowbrook. Emma couldn't help but feel a mixture of excitement and nervousness as the day approached.

The day of their long-awaited meeting finally arrived. Emma walked into the café, scanning the crowd in search of Alex. Suddenly, she spotted a tall, bearded man with a friendly smile waving at her. It was Alex. As they embraced, their connection felt genuine, just as it had online. He was even cuter in person than his pictures online. It was a case of **love at first sight**.

As they sat down, **sipping** their coffees, Emma and Alex reminisced about their online conversations, realizing how much they had in common. They laughed, shared stories, and even discovered new interests they could explore together.

Days turned into weeks, weeks into months, and Emma and Alex's bond continued to grow stronger. They embarked on countless adventures, exploring the beauty of nature, capturing stunning photographs, and making cherished memories. Their love story had begun online, but it had transcended the digital world and transformed into a beautiful reality.

Through online dating, Emma had found her perfect match. She had learned that true love knows no boundaries, not even those of a computer screen. It was a reminder that sometimes, taking a **leap of faith** and venturing into the unknown could lead to the most incredible journeys of all.

Vocabulary

close-knit: A group of people with strong relationships.

captivating: Able to attract, and hold interest.

genuine: Real; sincere.

blossoming: Growing.

love at first sight: A feeling of instant connection to someone, on the first meeting.

sipping: Drinking something slowly.

leap of faith: Doing something where the outcome is unknowable.

Comprehension Questions

1. Why did Emma find it difficult to meet a romantic partner?
2. Did Emma talk extensively to many people on the dating apps?
3. Did Emma and Alex get to know each other well before meeting in person?
4. Was Emma disappointed when she met Alex at the coffee shop?
5. How long did they end up dating?

Answers

1. She found it difficult because she lived in such a close-knit community.
2. No, it seems like she focused on one guy, Alex.
3. Yes, they messaged daily about their hopes, fears, and dreams.
4. No, she wasn't. She thought he was even cuter than his pictures online.
5. They dated for months, and are still together when the story ends.

Summarize the Story

Using 1-2 sentences, summarize the story. Include only the main details and key events.

Summary:

New Words

Write down any new words that you learned from this story. Consider writing them in a vocabulary notebook or making some flashcards for further review.

-
-
-

Let's Talk More

1. Have you ever tried online dating? How did it go?
2. What are some ways that people can meet romantic partners, not online?
3. Are there any dangers to online dating?
4. Can you imagine life even 20 years ago, before online dating apps?

The Canucks Game

There was a guy named Alex who moved to Vancouver to study English. Alex had recently moved to the city and was excited to **immerse** himself in the **local culture**. He had heard a lot about ice hockey and how passionate Canadians were about the sport. So when he found out that the Vancouver Canucks, the local hockey team, had a game coming up, Alex knew he had to experience it firsthand.

With great anticipation, Alex bought a ticket to the Canucks game at Rogers Arena. He arrived early at the arena, feeling a mix of nervousness and excitement. The atmosphere was **electric** as fans clad in blue and green jerseys filled the stadium. The sound of cheerful conversations, laughter, and the smell of freshly made popcorn filled the air.

As Alex took his seat, he noticed the giant scoreboard above the ice rink, displaying the team's logo with pride. The lights **dimmed**, and the crowd erupted in cheers as the players skated onto the ice. The game began, and the speed and skill of the players amazed Alex. He could feel the intensity of the game, and it was infectious.

Throughout the game, Alex couldn't help but join in the chants and cheers with the other fans. He learned the popular chants like "Go Canucks, Go!" and "Let's go, Vancouver!" It didn't matter if he didn't understand every word; the energy in the arena carried him along.

During the intermission, Alex decided to explore the concourse. They discovered various food stands offering classic Canadian treats like poutine and maple syrup-flavored donuts. Alex indulged in a delicious hot dog, feeling grateful for this wonderful cultural experience. Of course, he bought a couple of very expensive beers as well.

As the game continued, the Canucks scored a goal, and the crowd erupted in an explosion of joy. The unity felt in that moment was incredible. Alex found himself high-fiving strangers, connected by his shared love for the team.

Even though the Canucks didn't win that particular game, Alex left the arena with a **newfound** appreciation for ice hockey and the Vancouver Canucks. He felt a sense of belonging and understood why hockey was such an **integral** part of Canadian culture.

Walking back home, Alex couldn't help but **reflect** on the amazing experience he had just had. He realized that attending a Vancouver Canucks game was more than just watching a sport; it was about being part of a community, celebrating together, and embracing **the spirit of the game**.

From that day forward, Alex continued to support the Canucks, attending games whenever possible. He made new friends, bonded over shared victories and defeats, and became a true fan of the team. The Vancouver Canucks had not only given Alex a memorable evening but also a lifelong passion for ice hockey and a deep love for his new home.

Vocabulary

immerse: Involve oneself deeply in something.

local culture: The way of life in a certain location.

electric: Exciting; thrilling.

dimmed: Became less bright.

newfound: Recently discovered.

integral: Very important; key.

reflect: Think back upon something.

the spirit of the game: Sportsmanship; fair play, playing for the love of the game.

Comprehension Questions

1. Did Alex know a lot about hockey before moving to Vancouver?
2. What was the atmosphere like at the arena?
3. What are some examples of unity amongst the fans?
4. Do you think Alex will be a Canucks fan for life?
5. Do Canadians love hockey?

Answers
1. No, he didn't.
2. It was very exciting—lots of sights, smells, sounds, and Canucks fans.
3. They were united in their chants and cheers, as well as when the Canucks scored a goal.
4. Yes, most likely! He watched games after that whenever possible.
5. Yes, Canadians are very passionate about hockey.

Summarize the Story

Using 1-2 sentences, summarize the story. Include only the main details and key events.

Summary:

New Words

Write down any new words that you learned from this story. Consider writing them in a vocabulary notebook or making some flashcards for further review.

-
-
-

Let's Talk More
1. Have you ever been to a professional hockey game? What was that experience like? If you haven't, you can talk about an experience at another sport.
2. Do you think that sport can positively unite countries?
3. Do professional athletes get paid too much money in your opinion?
4. If you have/had children, would you ever encourage them to try to become professional athletes?
5. Do you think sports like hockey or American football are too violent?

Who is That?

Jay was at the movie theater with his two friends, Keith and Tony. They were going to watch the new Superman movie. It was popular and difficult to get tickets to. But his friend Keith **reserved** some online for them. He was good at doing stuff like that.

They had to wait in line at the theater to **pick up** their tickets. It was a Friday night, so it was quite busy. Just in front of them was a group of women around the same age as them. Jay noticed one of the women in front of him. She had long, beautiful hair and was wearing nice jeans and a sweater. "Who is that?," he thought to himself, "She is beautiful."

Jay was **lost in his own thoughts** about the woman in front of him and not listening to his friends. Keith and Tony laughed loudly at a joke, and the woman turned around to see who was laughing. She looked at all of them and then smiled at Jay. They made **eye contact,** and he smiled back. Jay wanted to talk to her, but he was nervous so he didn't.

They finally got their tickets and went to the **concession** to get some drinks and popcorn for the movie. Jay told his friends about this beautiful woman. They said that he should go say hi, but he knew that he never would! He was too **shy** to do that kind of thing. His friends said he was making a mistake and that he'd regret it.

They got their popcorn and drinks, and Tony grabbed a napkin. He asked someone who worked at the movie theater for a pen. Jay thought it was strange to be asking for a pen at the movie theater but didn't pay attention to him. Tony asked Jay to show him which woman he thought was beautiful. He pointed her out, sitting on a bench, waiting for the movie to start. Tony walked over and handed her the napkin.

Jay said, "TONY! What did you do?" Tony said, "I wrote down your name and phone number on the napkin and said that you wanted to go on a date with her. You're welcome! Hahahaha!"

Then, they had to go into the movie theater. They sat down, and Jay's phone **buzzed**. It was the woman, introducing herself. She said that they should go for a drink after the movie. Jay quickly said yes, and they made plans to meet at a pub that was very close to the movie theater. Jay was excited and could hardly concentrate on the movie! It seemed to go on forever.

Vocabulary

reserved: Booked ahead of time. For example, tickets or a table at a restaurant.

pick up: Get something or someone from somewhere.

lost in his own thoughts: Thinking about something, not paying attention to other people; daydreaming.

eye contact: When two people look directly into each other's eyes.

concession: A place to buy snacks or drinks at a movie theater or sports event.

shy: Finds it difficult to talk to people, especially people they don't know well.

buzzed: Made a sound or vibration, usually refers to a cellphone when you get a message.

Comprehension Questions

1. Who got the tickets for them?
2. Who noticed the beautiful woman?
3. When did Jay first notice her?
4. How did Jay get her phone number?
5. Is Jay going to meet the woman?
6. Do you think that Tony is a good friend? Why?

Answers

1. Keith reserved the tickets.
2. Jay noticed the woman.
3. He noticed her when they were standing in line at the movie theater.
4. Tony gave Jay's phone number to the woman on a napkin.
5. Yes, Jay is going to meet the woman after the movie.
6. (many answers possible).

Summarize the Story

Using 1-2 sentences, summarize the story. Include only the main details and key events.

Summary:

New Words

Write down any new words that you learned from this story. Consider writing them in a vocabulary notebook or making some flashcards for further review.

-
-
-

Let's Talk More

1. Would you ever do something similar to what Tony did?
2. How would you react if someone approached you like that in a public place?
3. Have you met a boyfriend or girlfriend on a dating app? How about "in real life?"
4. What are some movie theater etiquette rules (how to be polite) in your country?
5. Do you prefer to watch movies at home or in a movie theater? Why?

A Hiking Misadventure

Once upon a time, in a small town nestled between towering mountains, there lived a curious and adventurous young man named Jack. Jack had always been fascinated by nature and the great outdoors, so he decided to **embark** on a hiking adventure one sunny morning.

Armed with a backpack filled with snacks, a map, and his trusty compass, Jack set off on a trail that wound through the dense forest. The air was crisp, and the sound of birds chirping added to the **tranquil ambiance**. Jack was thrilled to explore new paths, discover hidden waterfalls, and breathe in the fresh mountain air.

As Jack ventured deeper into the woods, he became **enthralled** by the beauty surrounding him. The tall trees seemed to whisper ancient secrets, and the sunlight peeked through the canopy, creating a magical dance of light and shadows. However, in his excitement, Jack failed to notice that he had **deviated** from the main trail.

After a while, Jack realized that he couldn't find any familiar landmarks. His heart raced as panic began to set in. The forest suddenly seemed unfamiliar and vast. He checked his map, but the unfamiliar paths and dense foliage made it difficult to determine his exact location. The once inviting woods now felt like a maze closing in on him.

Trying to keep a level head, Jack remembered the lessons he had learned about staying calm when lost. He knew that panicking would only make matters worse. He took a deep breath and decided to retrace his steps, hoping to find the trail he had strayed from.

With each step, the forest seemed to grow darker and more intimidating. Jack's mind played tricks on him as the **rustling** leaves and distant animal sounds heightened his sense of unease. He tried to ignore the fear and focused on the task at hand.

Suddenly, Jack heard a faint sound in the distance. It was a gentle stream, babbling through the forest. His spirits lifted as he followed the sound, hoping it would lead him to a familiar place. And sure enough, after what felt like an eternity, he stumbled upon the familiar path, bathed in sunlight, with the stream flowing beside it.

Relieved, Jack let out a sigh of relief and **thanked his lucky stars**. He had learned a valuable lesson about the importance of staying alert and following the trail markers. As he made his way back to the town, he marveled at the beauty of the forest but also respected its unpredictable nature.

From that day forward, Jack never went hiking without a hiking buddy or a detailed trail guide. He shared his story with others, emphasizing the importance of being prepared and staying calm in challenging situations. And whenever he looked at the mountains, he couldn't help but feel a sense of gratitude for the adventure that had taught him so much.

Please remember Jack's story as you embark on your own journeys. Stay **vigilant**, be prepared, and most importantly, stay calm when faced with unexpected challenges. Happy hiking!

Vocabulary

embark: Start; begin.

tranquil ambiance: Peaceful, quiet surroundings.

enthralled: Deeply fascinated.

deviated: Moved or strayed from the original plan.

rustling: Moving.

thanked his lucky stars: Was appreciative of his good luck.

vigilant: Aware; focused.

Comprehension Questions

1. Was Jack prepared for the hike?
2. How did he get lost?
3. How did his feeling about the forest change once he realized he was lost?
4. How did he find his way back?
5. What lesson did Jack learn from this experience?

Answers
1. He was partly prepared—he had snacks, a map, and a compass.
2. He got lost because he was paying attention to other things—not where he was going.
3. Once he got lost, the forest changed from a beautiful place to one that was scary and intimidating.
4. He found a stream, which led him back to the hiking trail.
5. Jack now always goes hiking with a friend and has a detailed trail guide.

Summarize the Story

Using 1-2 sentences, summarize the story. Include only the main details and key events.
Summary:

New Words

Write down any new words that you learned from this story. Consider writing them in a vocabulary notebook or making some flashcards for further review.

-
-
-

Let's Talk More
1. Have you ever gotten lost? Describe that experience.
2. Have you heard about the 10 essentials for when you go hiking? What are they? Look it up on Google if you don't know.
3. How well do you prepare for a hike or walk?
4. Are you the type of person who likes adventures like this? Or, do you prefer a calmer kind of life?
5. Do you think it would be easy to get lost like this person did when out hiking?

A Trip to Europe

Once upon a time, in a small town nestled in the countryside, there lived a young woman named Sarah. She had always dreamt of going on a grand adventure, exploring new places and experiencing different cultures. Finally, the day came when Sarah decided to turn her dream into reality by going on a trip to Europe.

Excitement filled Sarah's heart as she boarded the plane bound for her first destination, Paris, France. Stepping off the plane, she was greeted by the magnificent Eiffel Tower, standing tall against the backdrop of a clear blue sky. Sarah couldn't help but feel **awe-struck** by its **grandeur.**

With a map in hand and a determined spirit, Sarah set off to explore the charming streets of Paris. She walked along the Seine River, taking in the sights of **quaint** cafés and art galleries. The **aroma** of freshly baked croissants and the sound of laughter filled the air. Sarah felt like she had stepped into a dream.

From Paris, Sarah embarked on a train journey to Rome, Italy. The city was a living testament to ancient history. Sarah stood before the Colosseum, imagining the gladiator battles that once took place within its walls. She tossed a coin into the Trevi Fountain, making a wish for her journey to be filled with unforgettable memories.

Next, Sarah found herself in Barcelona, Spain. The vibrant city pulsated with energy. She strolled along Las Ramblas, where street performers entertained passersby with their mesmerizing skills. Sarah indulged in **delectable** tapas and danced to the rhythm of flamenco music, embracing the lively spirit of the city.

Sarah's adventure continued as she hopped on a train to Amsterdam, Netherlands. The picturesque canals and charming windmills took her breath away. She pedaled on a bicycle, joining the locals in their preferred mode of transportation. Sarah visited the famous Van Gogh Museum and marveled at the artist's masterpieces, each stroke of paint telling a story.

As her journey drew to a close, Sarah arrived in London, England. She explored the historic landmarks, including the majestic Buckingham Palace and the iconic Tower

Bridge. Sarah savored afternoon tea, complete with scones, clotted cream, and delicious finger sandwiches. The city's rich history and diverse culture left a lasting impression on her.

With a heavy heart, Sarah **bid farewell** to Europe and returned home. Her trip had been a magnificent adventure, filled with incredible sights, delicious food, and unforgettable experiences. But most importantly, Sarah had discovered the beauty of diversity and the joy of stepping out of her comfort zone.

As Sarah reminisced about her European journey, she realized that traveling had opened her mind and broadened her perspective. It taught her to embrace new cultures and appreciate the beauty of the world. Inspired, Sarah began planning her next adventure, eager to explore more of the world and continue her **journey of self-discovery**.

Vocabulary

awe-struck: Filled with wonder or amazement.

grandeur: Impressiveness, regarding appearance.

quaint: Unusual; old-fashioned.

delectable: Delicious.

bid farewell: Said goodbye.

journey of self-discovery: A pilgrimage or trip where someone wants to learn something about themselves.

Comprehension Questions

1. How many countries did she go to?
2. Where did Sarah enjoy food and dancing?
3. How did she feel about her trip ending?
4. Do you think she probably wants to go back to Europe?
5. Did she go to Europe for one specific thing (the history, or the food, for example)?

Answers
1. She went to 5 countries.
2. She enjoyed the food and dancing in Barcelona, Spain.
3. She had a heavy heart (sadness) about her trip to Europe ending.
4. She likely wants to go back to Europe. It seems like she loved it.
5. No, she explored different things in each country she went to.

Summarize the Story

Using 1-2 sentences, summarize the story. Include only the main details and key events.
Summary:

New Words

Write down any new words that you learned from this story. Consider writing them in a vocabulary notebook or making some flashcards for further review.

-
-
-

Let's Talk More
1. Have you ever been on a big vacation? Where did you go?
2. What do you like to see or do on vacation? Do you focus on the food, the history, relaxing, etc.?
3. Have you ever had a journey or self-discovery? What did you learn about yourself?
4. Is there a place in the world that you'd like to go to? Why?
5. What do you think about going on vacation alone? Do you think it'd be fun, challenging, or maybe both?

Max and Emily

Once upon a time in a small town, there lived a young girl named Emily. Emily had a loyal and loving companion named Max, her faithful golden retriever. Max had been a part of Emily's life since she was a little girl, and they had shared countless joyful moments.

Max was not just a dog; he was Emily's best friend. They explored the neighborhood, **played fetch** in the park, and even cuddled up for bedtime stories. Max always seemed to understand Emily's emotions, providing comfort and **unconditional love** when she needed it most.

One sunny day, as Emily and Max were enjoying their usual afternoon walk, tragedy struck. Max suddenly collapsed, struggling to breathe. Alarmed and filled with worry, Emily quickly rushed him to the nearest veterinarian. The vet examined Max carefully and delivered heartbreaking news: Max's health had **deteriorated** rapidly, and there was little they could do to save him. Emily's heart sank with despair upon hearing the news.

Emily returned home, her heart heavy with grief. She sat on her bed, surrounded by Max's favorite toys and his worn-out dog bed. Tears streamed down her face as she **reminisced** about the countless memories she had shared with her beloved friend.

Days turned into weeks, and the emptiness in Emily's heart remained. She missed the sound of Max's paws on the floor, his wagging tail, and his warm presence beside her. Every corner of the house held a memory of him, and his absence felt unbearable.

Emily's parents understood her pain and decided to help her cope with the loss. They suggested creating a memory box for Max, filled with photographs, drawings, and heartfelt letters expressing their love and gratitude for him. They spent hours reminiscing about the happy moments they had shared with Max and remembering his playful antics.

Through the process of remembering and honoring Max, Emily and her family **found solace** in the memories they had created together. They celebrated Max's life, cherishing the love and joy he had brought into their lives. The memory box became a precious treasure, reminding them that Max would forever remain in their hearts.

As time passed, Emily's sorrow slowly transformed into acceptance and gratitude for the beautiful moments she had shared with Max. Though she missed him dearly, she knew that Max would want her to find happiness and love again.

One day, Emily's parents surprised her with a new puppy named Buddy. With a wagging tail and eyes full of curiosity, Buddy brought a newfound energy and excitement into their lives. Emily welcomed Buddy with open arms, understanding that while Max could never be replaced, her heart had room for new connections and love.

Emily and Buddy grew together, building their own unique bond. They embarked on new adventures, exploring the world with the same spirit of joy and love that Max had taught them. Max's memory continued to live on in their hearts, guiding them through life's ups and downs.

In the end, Emily realized that although saying goodbye to Max had been painful, his presence had forever changed her life for the better. Through love and memories, Max had taught her the true meaning of companionship and unconditional love, lessons that would stay with her forever.

And so, the tale of Emily, Max, and Buddy reminds us that even when we experience loss, the memories we create and the love we share can carry us through the darkest times, **illuminating** our path toward healing and happiness.

Vocabulary

played fetch: A game that humans and dogs play. The human throws a stick, the dog runs to get it and then brings it back.

unconditional love: Love that doesn't depend on anything.

deteriorated: Got worse.

reminisced: Remembered happy memories.

found solace: Found comfort.

illuminating: Lighting.

Comprehension Questions
1. Does Emily love Max?
2. Did Emily have Max for a long time?
3. What did Emily's family do to remember Max?
4. Who is Buddy?
5. Was Buddy going to replace Max?

Answers
1. Yes, she loves him. He is her best friend.
2. Yes, she did.
3. They made a memory box for Max.
4. Buddy is the new dog that Emily's parents got.
5. No. No dog could replace Max. But Emily could also love Buddy.

Summarize the Story

Using 1-2 sentences, summarize the story. Include only the main details and key events.

Summary:

New Words

Write down any new words that you learned from this story. Consider writing them in a vocabulary notebook or making some flashcards for further review.

-
-

Let's Talk More
1. Have you ever had a pet that you really loved? Describe them.
2. Do people spend too much time and money on pets?
3. Should we euthanize pets that are very sick, or let them live as long as possible?
4. How can you choose a good pet that's suitable for you?

The New Italian Restaurant

Sam and Tony were out for a walk in their neighborhood when they noticed a big line up. "I wonder why they're lining up? Hmmm. It looks like a new restaurant," said Tony. They asked someone in the line what they were waiting for. The person said that it's a new Italian restaurant, Luigi's. They had become popular because of a **review** in **the Vancouver Sun**. The person reviewing the restaurant loved it and said that it was now the best Italian in Vancouver. This made everyone want to try it as well!

Sam and Tony decided to **check it out** on Friday night. Tony called to make a reservation, but Luigi's said that they don't take reservations. They would just have to line up and hopefully get a seat. Sam guessed that it wouldn't be that busy if they went earlier, so they decided to go at 5:00.

Friday night came, and they walked over to Luigi's. They got there at 5:00, and there was already a line up of about 20 people. They decided to wait. It would probably be worth it. Sam and Tony chatted with people while they waited. Everyone was excited to try the food. Some people were going to try the pasta while others wanted pizza. Luigi's used a brick oven for making pizza, just like in Italy.

Finally, after about an hour, they got a table. Sam ordered a glass of white wine while Tony went with red. The waiter also brought them some bread and oil and balsamic vinegar to dip it in. They ordered two things to share: spaghetti & meatballs and a **margherita pizza**. They liked to try a bit of everything, so they usually ordered things to share. The food came quickly, which surprised them because the restaurant was **packed.**

The wait was worth it. It was the best Italian food either of them had ever tried. Although it was expensive, it was worth it. Lining up for an hour was also worth it! The food was so delicious. For dessert, they had homemade **tiramisu** and some Italian coffee. When the meal was done, they paid the bill and left a generous **tip**. Sam said, "Tomorrow night? Same time, same place?" He was joking, but Tony said, "YES! I want to try everything."

Vocabulary

review: An opinion about something. In this case, about Luigi's restaurant.

the Vancouver Sun: A newspaper in Vancouver.

check it out: Go to, look at, examine, etc. In this case, go to the restaurant.

margherita pizza: Pizza with tomato sauce, basil and mozzarella cheese.

packed: Filled with people; completely full.

tiramisu: An Italian dessert.

tip: Money someone gives for good service at a restaurant, hotel, hair shop, etc.

Comprehension Questions

1. Why is Luigi's so busy?
2. Does the restaurant take reservations?
3. When did they decide to go there?
4. Why did Sam and Tony go there at 5:00?
5. What did they order?
6. Did they like the food?

Answers

1. It's because of a good review in the *Vancouver Sun*.
2. They don't take reservations.
3. They decided to go on Friday for dinner.
4. They thought it wouldn't be so busy at 5:00 (instead of later).
5. They ordered wine, pizza, pasta, tiramisu and coffee.
6. They loved it. They want to go back soon!

Summarize the Story

Using 1-2 sentences, summarize the story. Include only the main details and key events.

Summary:

New Words

Write down any new words that you learned from this story. Consider writing them in a vocabulary notebook or making some flashcards for further review.

-
-
-

Let's Talk More

1. Have you ever waited in a long line at a restaurant? Was it worth it?
2. What's the best meal you've ever had at a restaurant? Was it a very expensive place?
3. Do you like Italian food? Why or why not?
4. What's your favorite kind of food to eat in a restaurant? Why?
5. Do you pay attention to how much things cost when you go out to eat? Or, do you just order whatever you want?

Ice Fishing in Manitoba

In the vast and frozen land of Manitoba, Canada lived a young man named Ethan. Ethan had always been fascinated by the icy wonders that surrounded him. He often heard tales of **ice fishing,** a popular activity in his community, and longed to experience it for himself.

One winter morning, Ethan woke up to find a **pristine** white blanket of snow covering the ground. The temperature had dropped significantly, and the nearby lakes had frozen over, signaling the perfect opportunity for him to fulfill his ice fishing dreams.

Excitedly, Ethan packed his warmest clothes, grabbed his fishing gear, and set off toward the frozen lake. As he arrived, he couldn't help but marvel at the winter landscape. The towering trees stood tall, their branches dusted with snow, while the sunlight danced on the sparkling ice.

Ethan carefully walked onto the frozen lake, ensuring each step was secure. He found a cozy spot and began to drill a hole through the ice. The sound of the drill echoed across the lake, making him feel like an explorer on a grand adventure.

With his fishing rod in hand, Ethan settled down, patiently waiting for a fish to bite. The air was crisp, and he could feel the cold seep into his bones. But the anticipation kept him warm. He watched as the line disappeared into the icy depths below, hoping for a tug that would signal a catch.

Time passed, and Ethan's patience started to waver. Just as he was about to give up, he felt a sudden jerk on his fishing line. His heart raced with excitement as he swiftly reeled in the fish. To his amazement, a beautiful **walleye** emerged from the icy hole.

Overjoyed, Ethan carefully removed the hook from the fish's mouth and marveled at its shimmering scales. He couldn't help but appreciate the stunning creature that lay before him. Grateful for the experience, he gently released the walleye back into the water, knowing that it would continue its journey beneath the frozen surface.

As the day went on, Ethan had more success with his ice fishing endeavors. Each catch brought him a sense of fulfillment and wonder. He even met fellow ice fishermen, who shared stories of their adventures and tips for success.

As the sun began to set, casting **hues** of orange and pink across the **horizon**, Ethan knew it was time to leave. Reluctantly, he packed up his gear, taking one last look at the frozen lake that had provided him with an unforgettable experience.

With a smile on his face, Ethan **trudged** through the snow, feeling a sense of accomplishment and connection to the winter world around him. He knew that he would always cherish the memories he had made while ice fishing in Manitoba.

And so, as the stars twinkled above, Ethan walked home, his heart filled with the beauty of nature and the joy of a dream fulfilled. Little did he know that this would be the first of many adventures on the ice, as he had discovered a love for ice fishing that would continue to warm his spirit for years to come.

Vocabulary

ice fishing: Catching fish under the ice by drilling a hole.

pristine: Untouched; unspoiled.

walleye: A kind of freshwater fish.

hues: Shades of color.

horizon: The line where the Earth and the sky appear to meet.

trudged: Walked slowly.

Comprehension Questions

1. Is Ethan new to Canada?
2. Do you think that Ethan fishes in the summertime?
3. Did Ethan give up hope on catching a fish?
4. Did he eat the fish he caught for dinner?
5. Will he go ice fishing again?

Answers
1. No, it seems like he's been living in Manitoba for a while. He's just never been ice fishing before.
2. He likely fishes in the summer. He has all the equipment and seems to know how to fish.
3. Yes, a little bit. His patience started to waver.
4. No, he released it back into the lake.
5. Yes, he will have many more fishing adventures on the ice.

Summarize the Story

Using 1-2 sentences, summarize the story. Include only the main details and key events.
Summary:

New Words

Write down any new words that you learned from this story. Consider writing them in a vocabulary notebook or making some flashcards for further review.

-
-
-

Let's Talk More
1. Have you ever been fishing? What was that experience like?
2. Do you think ice fishing would be fun? Why or why not?
3. Do you prefer to be somewhere hot or cold?
4. Is fishing cruel to animals? What about catching them and then releasing them back, instead of eating them?
5. What are some other hobbies or sports that you can only do in certain climates?

Getting Caught

Once upon a time, in a small town called Willowbrook, there was a **diligent** student named Emily. She was known for her exceptional academic performance and had always been praised for her honesty and integrity. However, as the final exams approached, Emily found herself overwhelmed with stress and anxiety. The pressure to excel in every subject had started to take a toll on her.

One day, while studying in the library, Emily noticed a fellow classmate named Alex. Alex was **notorious** for his laziness and lack of interest in academics. He always seemed to find shortcuts to avoid studying. Intrigued, Emily approached him and asked if he had any tips to cope with the mounting stress.

With a mischievous smile, Alex leaned in and whispered, "I have a secret method that guarantees success on any exam. All you need is a small cheat sheet hidden in your pencil case. No one will ever notice."

Emily hesitated at first, but the temptation of an easy solution overwhelmed her. She decided to give it a try. Late that night, she **meticulously** prepared a cheat sheet with all the answers she thought she might need.

The next day, as the exam began, Emily took a deep breath and placed the cheat sheet inside her pencil case. However, as she started to write, her heart raced, and her **conscience** weighed heavy on her. Each glance at the cheat sheet brought a pang of guilt. She knew deep down that cheating was wrong, no matter the circumstances.

Just as she was about to surrender to her guilt and put the cheat sheet away, the invigilator, Ms. Thompson, noticed a piece of paper sticking out from Emily's pencil case. Suspicion grew on her face as she approached Emily's desk. The room fell silent as all eyes turned toward her.

Ms. Thompson sternly asked, "Emily, what is that paper in your pencil case?"

Emily's face flushed with embarrassment as she realized her moment of weakness was about to be exposed. She took a deep breath, her voice trembling, and confessed, "It's a **cheat sheet**, Ms. Thompson. I made a terrible mistake."

The entire room gasped in disbelief. Ms. Thompson, disappointed but determined to teach Emily a valuable lesson, took the cheat sheet and handed it to the principal. Emily was asked to leave the examination hall, and her paper would be marked as a zero.

Feeling **humiliated**, Emily realized the consequences of her actions. She had not only let herself down but had also betrayed the trust of her teachers, classmates, and most importantly, herself. As she walked home that day, tears streaming down her face, she vowed never to compromise her integrity again.

In the days that followed, Emily faced the consequences of her decision. She retaught herself the material she had tried to cheat on, spending countless hours studying late into the night. She even sought help from her teachers to make amends and learn from her mistake.

Over time, Emily's hard work and determination paid off. Although she couldn't change her past, she used her experience to grow stronger and became an **advocate** for academic integrity. She shared her story with her classmates and stressed the importance of honesty, reminding them that true success comes from dedication and perseverance.

Vocabulary

diligent: Showing care about one's work.

notorious: Famous or well-known for something.

meticulously: Doing something carefully, paying close attention to detail.

conscience: An inner feeling or voice about what is right.

cheat sheet: A small piece of paper that helps someone cheat on an exam.

humiliated: Very embarrassed.

advocate: A person who publicly supports a cause of some kind.

Comprehension Questions

1. How are Emily and Alex different from each other?
2. Why was Emily tempted to cheat?
3. Why was Emily humiliated?
4. What is academic integrity?

Answers

1. Emily is a good student, while Alex is known for being lazy.
2. She was tempted because she was under a lot of pressure to do well in all of her classes.
3. She was humiliated because her teacher caught her cheating.
4. Academic integrity is morality, as it relates to studies (not cheating!).

Summarize the Story

Using 1-2 sentences, summarize the story. Include only the main details and key events.
Summary:

New Words

Write down any new words that you learned from this story. Consider writing them in a vocabulary notebook or making some flashcards for further review.

-
-

Let's Talk More

1. Have you ever been tempted to cheat on something? Did you end up doing it?
2. Should punishment be lenient or harsh for something like this story?
3. Do cheaters hurt themselves? Give your opinion.
4. What would you do if you saw a classmate cheating on a test?
5. Does everyone cheat on things like taxes?

Learning to Play Tennis

Emily was always fascinated by sports, and she dreamt of becoming a skilled tennis player. One sunny day, as she passed by the local tennis court, she saw a group of people playing and having fun. Their energetic movements and the sound of the ball hitting the racket excited her. That's when Emily decided to **embark** on her journey to learn how to play tennis.

With **determination** in her heart, Emily approached the coach at the tennis court, Mr. Johnson. She shyly asked him if he would be willing to teach her how to play tennis. Mr. Johnson was delighted to see Emily's enthusiasm and agreed to be her coach.

They started their first lesson by teaching Emily the basic rules of tennis. Mr. Johnson explained that the **objective** was to hit the ball over the net and inside the boundary lines. He showed her the proper grip and how to position her feet.

Emily practiced diligently, hitting the ball back and forth with Mr. Johnson. At first, she struggled to control the racket and make accurate shots. But she didn't give up. She knew that learning something new takes time and patience.

As weeks turned into months, Emily's skills improved. She began to understand the different types of shots like forehand, backhand, and volley. She learned how to serve the ball and how to move swiftly around the court. Mr. Johnson encouraged her every step of the way, praising her effort and progress.

Emily also started participating in friendly matches with other beginners. She faced some tough opponents, but she never let failure discourage her. Instead, she saw each match as an opportunity to learn and grow. She analyzed her mistakes and worked on improving her weaknesses.

Over time, Emily's hard work paid off. She became more confident on the tennis court, winning matches against players who were once better than her. Her dedication and passion for the game **propelled** her forward.

One day, Emily received an invitation to compete in a local tennis tournament. Excited and nervous, she accepted the challenge. The tournament was a big test of her skills and mental strength. Emily faced strong opponents, but she played with determination and a smile on her face. She put all her training and knowledge into practice.

To her surprise, Emily reached the final match. It was a tough battle, but Emily fought hard and stayed focused. Finally, the moment arrived. Emily won the final point, and the crowd **erupted** in applause. She couldn't believe it—she had won the tournament! It was a remarkable achievement for someone who had started as a beginner not too long ago.

Emily's journey to learn tennis taught her valuable lessons about **perseverance**, dedication, and the joy of pursuing one's passion. She realized that success is not measured by the trophies won but by the growth and progress made along the way.

From that day forward, Emily continued to play tennis, always striving to improve and reach new heights. She became an inspiration to other aspiring tennis players, showing them that with determination and hard work, dreams can come true.

Vocabulary

embark: Begin something.

determination: A strong intention to do something.

objective: Aim or goal.

propelled: Pushed forward.

erupted: Explode with noise (can also refer to a volcano).

perseverance: Doing something despite difficulty.

Comprehension Questions

1. Did Emily like sports?
2. Who is Mr. Johnson?
3. How good of a student of tennis was Emily?
4. What is Emily's attitude towards losing a tennis match?
5. Was it surprising that Emily won the tournament she entered?

Answers
1. Yes, she enjoyed lots of sports.
2. Mr. Johnson is Emily's tennis coach.
3. She was an excellent student of tennis. She worked very hard to improve her skills.
4. She has a good attitude towards losing. She just sees it as an opportunity to learn from her mistakes.
5. Yes, it was quite surprising since it was her first one.

Summarize the Story

Using 1-2 sentences, summarize the story. Include only the main details and key events.
Summary:

New Words

Write down any new words that you learned from this story. Consider writing them in a vocabulary notebook or making some flashcards for further review.

-
-
-

Let's Talk More
1. Have you ever worked hard to learn something new? What was it?
2. How do you view failure?
3. When learning something new, what are some important qualities to have if you want to eventually be very good at it?
4. Have you ever played tennis or another racquet sport? Did you enjoy it?
5. Is winning, or the journey along the way most important to you in competitive activities that you do?

A Summer BBQ

Summertime in Canada's capital city, Ottawa is beautiful. The days are long and the weather is hot and sunny. People that have houses with **backyards** love to have summer BBQs with family and friends. People without yards often take a portable BBQ to the park. It was one of Ted's favourite things to do in the summer.

Ted decided to have a BBQ for his birthday on June 3rd. It was a Saturday which was perfect because most people would be free. He invited all of his coworkers since he worked with only a few people. He also invited some neighbors that he liked and a few friends. Plus, his sister and her family too. Most people said that they could come so there would be about 25 in total. He was happy that most people agreed to come.

He asked everyone to bring a chair to sit on, some drinks and a side dish like potato chips, watermelon or salad. He planned to BBQ some chicken for the **meat eaters** and some tofu for the **vegans**. Ted bought lots of beer and made a big potato salad as well. He also bought some paper plates and cups, as well as **utensils** because he didn't want to wash dishes for 25 people! He didn't even have enough normal plates, cups and metal utensils for so many people.

On the morning of the party, he took out all of his outdoor chairs and BBQ from the garage. He got his biggest **cooler** and filled it with ice and beer. He **marinated** the chicken and tofu in some homemade BBQ sauce and put it back in the fridge. Plus, he cleaned the bathroom. All that was left was for the guests to arrive. He felt a little bit nervous because he hoped that everyone would have a fun time. But, he was also excited to see everyone and have some fun!

The guests began to arrive at 3:00, bringing lots of delicious food and drinks with them. Almost everyone knew each other already and they were having a great time. There was lots of conversation and laughing.

Once everyone was there, Ted turned on the BBQ and began cooking the chicken and tofu. The BBQ was a little bit hot and he was worried about the chicken burning but not being cooked on the inside, so he turned it down. Finally, it was done, and everyone grabbed a piece. The party was quiet as everyone was eating. It must have been delicious!

Vocabulary

summertime: Summer. In Canada, the months of June-August.

backyard: A place with grass behind a house.

meat eaters: People who eat meat like beef, pork, or chicken.

vegans: People who don't eat animal products.

utensils: Spoons, forks and knives.

cooler: A box to put ice and food/drinks in to keep things cold.

marinate: Put something like meat or tofu in sauce or spices before cooking for a few hours.

Comprehension Questions

1. Where do people like to BBQ in Ottawa?
2. What is Ted going to do for his birthday?
3. What did people have to bring to the party?
4. How many people are coming?
5. What did Ted make for the party?
6. Did everyone like the food?

Answers

1. People with big backyards like to BBQ there. However, people with very small or no backyards like to BBQ in public places like a park.
2. He is going to have a BBQ at his house.
3. They have to bring a chair, drinks and a side dish.
4. Around 25 people are coming to the party.
5. He made chicken, tofu and potato salad.
6. They probably liked it. Everyone was eating, and not talking.

Summarize the Story

Using 1-2 sentences, summarize the story. Include only the main details and key events.

Summary:

New Words

Write down any new words that you learned from this story. Consider writing them in a vocabulary notebook or making some flashcards for further review.

-
-
-

Let's Talk More

1. Have you ever been to a backyard BBQ party? What did you think about it?
2. Do you think that Ted prepared well for the party? Why or why not?
3. What are some things that make a good party? Have you ever been to a terrible party? What went wrong?
4. Do you enjoy cooking and eating outside?
5. Do people have yards like this in your country? What are some things people spend time doing in them?

The First Day of University

Sarah woke up with a mix of excitement and nervousness **fluttering** in her stomach. It was the first day of her university life. After years of hard work in high school, she finally earned a place at the **prestigious** Lynwood University. As she got ready, she couldn't help but wonder what the day had in store for her.

Sarah arrived on campus, marveling at the **grandeur** of the university buildings and the bustling atmosphere. Students from all walks of life hurried by, each with dreams and aspirations. The campus was **abuzz** with anticipation, as everyone seemed eager to start their academic journey.

Her first class was Introduction to Psychology, held in a large lecture hall. Sarah found a seat among her classmates, and the professor walked in, radiating knowledge and enthusiasm. He introduced himself and began the class by sharing fascinating insights into the human mind.

Throughout the day, Sarah attended various classes, each one offering a glimpse into a different field of study. From Chemistry to Literature, she was exposed to a world of knowledge that expanded her horizons. Sarah found herself engaged in discussions, jotting down notes, and making new friends with fellow students who shared her passion for learning.

During the lunch break, Sarah joined a group of students in the cafeteria. They exchanged stories and talked about their goals and ambitions. It was refreshing to be surrounded by like-minded individuals who were equally motivated to make the most of their university experience.

In the afternoon, Sarah attended an orientation session for a student club called "Global Minds." The club aimed to foster cultural understanding and encourage students to explore diverse perspectives. Intrigued by the club's mission, Sarah decided to join and contribute her ideas.

As the day drew to a close, Sarah reflected on her first day of university. It had been a whirlwind of new experiences, but she felt a sense of belonging and purpose. The challenges and opportunities that awaited her excited her even more.

Throughout her university journey, Sarah encountered both triumphs and setbacks. She faced difficult assignments, pulled all-nighters before exams, and learned to manage her time effectively. But she also made lifelong friends, **delved** into subjects she was passionate about, and discovered hidden talents within herself.

Through it all, Sarah embraced the essence of university life—the pursuit of knowledge, personal growth, and the joy of being part of a **vibrant** academic community. She realized that the first day of university was just the beginning of an incredible adventure, and she was determined to make the most of every moment. With renewed enthusiasm, she eagerly looked forward to the countless experiences that awaited her in the days and years to come.

Vocabulary

fluttering: Moving restlessly or anxiously.

prestigious: Describes something with high status.

grandeur: Impressive appearance.

abuzz: Describes a feeling of excitement.

delved: Explored.

vibrant: Full of energy and enthusiasm.

Comprehension Questions
1. Why was Sarah feeling nervous?
2. Did Sarah get good grades in high school?
3. What is Sarah's major?
4. Do you think she will finish her degree?
5. Did you focus only on academics?

Answers
1. She was feeling nervous because it was her first day of university.
2. Yes, she likely got good grades in high school because she's going to a prestigious university with a good reputation.
3. It doesn't say what her major is. She's taking a variety of courses in her first semester.
4. She will likely finish her degree. The story gives hints about that at the end.
5. No, she joined a club and spent time talking to the other students.

Summarize the Story

Using 1-2 sentences, summarize the story. Include only the main details and key events.
Summary:

New Words

Write down any new words that you learned from this story. Consider writing them in a vocabulary notebook or making some flashcards for further review.

-
-
-

Let's Talk More
1. Have you been to university or college? Did you enjoy your experience? (Or, do you plan to go?)
2. Is university necessary to get a good job in your country?
3. What do you think about schools where you learn a trade such as plumbing or fixing cars?
4. Do you think this story presents an idealized version of studying at a university?
5. What are some majors that can get someone a good job after they graduate? What are some majors that people consider to be a waste of time?

Making Homemade Pasta

Emma loved cooking and experimenting with different recipes. One day, she decided to try her hand at making homemade **ravioli**. Little did she know, this would be a culinary adventure that would teach her valuable lessons about patience, creativity, and the joy of sharing food with loved ones.

Emma started by gathering all the ingredients she needed: all-purpose flour, eggs, salt, olive oil, ricotta cheese, Parmesan cheese, spinach, and fresh basil. She cleared the kitchen counter, washed her hands, and put on her favorite apron, ready to **embark** on her homemade ravioli journey.

First, Emma prepared the pasta dough. She poured two cups of flour onto a wooden board, making a well in the center. In the well, she cracked two eggs and added a pinch of salt. With a fork, she whisked the eggs, gradually **incorporating** the flour until it formed a sticky dough. She then sprinkled some flour on the board and kneaded the dough until it became smooth and elastic.

Covering the dough with a clean cloth, Emma let it rest for about 30 minutes. During this time, she prepared the filling by wilting the spinach in a pan with a little olive oil and garlic. Once the spinach cooled down, she mixed it with ricotta cheese, Parmesan cheese, and freshly chopped basil. The **aroma** of the herbs filled the kitchen, making Emma even more excited to taste her homemade ravioli.

After the dough had rested, Emma divided it into smaller pieces and rolled each one into thin sheets using a rolling pin. She dusted the sheets with flour to prevent sticking and then spooned small mounds of the spinach and cheese filling onto one sheet, leaving space between them. Carefully, she covered the filling with another sheet of pasta and pressed around each mound to seal the edges, using a fork to create decorative ridges.

With all the ravioli prepared, Emma brought a large pot of water to a boil, adding a pinch of salt. She gently dropped the ravioli into the bubbling water, one by one, making sure not to overcrowd the pot. As the ravioli cooked, they **floated** to the surface, indicating they were ready to be served.

Using a slotted spoon, Emma carefully lifted the cooked ravioli from the pot and placed them onto serving plates. She drizzled a simple tomato sauce over the top, garnishing with a sprinkle of Parmesan cheese and a few fresh basil leaves.

As Emma sat down to enjoy her homemade ravioli, she couldn't help but marvel at the flavors she had created from scratch. The pasta was tender, the filling bursting with vibrant colors and tastes. She savored each bite, feeling **a sense of accomplishment** and pride.

But Emma's joy didn't end there. She called her friends and invited them to join her in the kitchen. With smiles on their faces, they gathered around the table, sharing stories and laughter while enjoying the delicious homemade ravioli together. Emma realized that cooking was not only about creating tasty meals but also about bringing people closer and creating lasting memories.

Vocabulary

ravioli: A kind of pasta with a savory filling in the middle.

embark: Begin; start.

incorporating: Mixing together.

aroma: Smell.

floated: Rested or moved to the surface of a liquid without sinking.

a sense of accomplishment: A feeling or pride at having done something.

Comprehension Questions

1. Has Emma made ravioli before?
2. Do you think homemade ravioli is easy to make?
3. Once you put the filling in the dough, can you eat the ravioli?
4. What kind of sauce did she put on the ravioli?
5. Did Emma eat the ravioli by herself?

Answers

1. No, she hasn't.
2. It doesn't seem that easy to make. There are a lot of steps in the process.
3. No, you have to cook the ravioli in boiling water before you eat them.
4. She used a simple tomato sauce with a bit of fresh basil.
5. No, she invited her friends over to share the ravioli with her.

Summarize the Story

Using 1-2 sentences, summarize the story. Include only the main details and key events.
Summary:

New Words

Write down any new words that you learned from this story. Consider writing them in a vocabulary notebook or making some flashcards for further review.

-
-
-

Let's Talk More

1. What do you like to cook?
2. Have you ever tried making homemade pasta? How did it go?
3. Have you ever cooked anything that took a long time and had many steps? Would you do it again?
4. Why does food bring people together?
5. What are some of the traditions surrounding food in your culture?

The English Test

Emily was a hardworking student who loved learning new things. Her favorite subject in school was English because she enjoyed reading books and writing stories.

One day, Emily's teacher announced that they would have an important English test the following week. Emily was excited and immediately started studying. She reviewed all the grammar rules, practiced writing essays, and even made flashcards to memorize new vocabulary words.

The day of the test finally arrived, and Emily felt confident as she sat down at her desk. However, as she read the first question, she realized that it was much more **challenging** than she had expected. She struggled to remember the correct grammar rules and couldn't find the right words to write her answers.

As the test went on, Emily's confidence began to **fade**. She felt frustrated and disappointed in herself. She knew she had studied hard, but she couldn't seem to recall the information when she needed it most. Doubt started to creep into her mind, and she worried about failing the test.

When the teacher collected the papers at the end of the test, Emily felt **a sinking feeling** in her stomach. She knew she had not performed well. The days that followed were filled with anxiety as she waited for the test results.

Finally, the day arrived when the teacher returned the graded tests to the students. As Emily received her paper, she hesitated to look at her score. With a deep breath, she opened it and saw a disappointing grade.

Emily's **heart sank**, but she knew she had to face the reality. She approached her teacher after class and asked for some guidance. The teacher noticed her determination and suggested that Emily join an after-school English club where she could practice speaking and writing in English.

Emily took the teacher's advice to heart and started attending the English club regularly. She worked hard to improve her language skills, asking for help whenever she needed it. She also realized that she needed to approach her studies differently. Instead of just memorizing rules and vocabulary, she focused on understanding and applying them in real-life situations.

Months went by, and Emily's hard work began to pay off. Her English skills started to improve, and she regained her confidence. She even began participating in class discussions and sharing her creative writing pieces.

The following year, when the English test was announced again, Emily felt nervous but determined. She had learned from her previous experience and knew that success wasn't just about getting a high score but also about **personal growth** and improvement.

This time, when Emily sat down for the test, she approached it with a calm and focused mindset. She carefully read each question, applied her knowledge, and answered to the best of her ability.

When the teacher returned the **graded** papers, Emily couldn't believe her eyes. She had not only passed the test but had also received an excellent score. She felt a sense of pride and accomplishment that she had never experienced before.

Vocabulary

challenging: Difficult.

fade: Get smaller or less.

a sinking feeling: A feeling of dread.

heart sank: To lose hope, or to feel disappointed.

personal growth: Improving habits or behavior.

graded: Scored.

Comprehension Questions

1. How did Emily feel before the test?
2. Do you think that Emily is a bad student?
3. When did she know that she didn't do well on the test?
4. Did Emily give up on English after not doing well on the test?
5. How does she view failure now?

Answers

1. She felt confident about the test.
2. No, she isn't a bad student.
3. She knew she didn't do well as she was writing the exam.
4. No, she asked her teacher for some advice and joined an English club.
5. She views failure as an opportunity for growth.

Summarize the Story

Using 1-2 sentences, summarize the story. Include only the main details and key events.

Summary:

New Words

Write down any new words that you learned from this story. Consider writing them in a vocabulary notebook or making some flashcards for further review.

-
-
-

Let's Talk More

1. Do you enjoy studying English? Why or why not?
2. What advice would you give someone who wants to improve their English skills?
3. Have you had any setbacks in life? How did you overcome them?
4. Are all failures an opportunity for growth?
5. Do you find tests helpful for learning new things?

Applying for University

Cindy is in grade 12, which is an important time for Canadian young people! It's the last year of high school, and students have to decide what they want to do when they **graduate**. There are lots of options! Getting a job, going to a **community college**, learning a **trade**, or university. Cindy got good grades in high school, so she decided to go to university. She eventually wanted to be a teacher, so this was necessary.

There are lots of universities in Canada, so she had to decide which ones to apply to. She lived in a small town in Manitoba, but she wanted to go to a bigger city. Her top two choices were Toronto and Vancouver so she applied to the University of Toronto, Simon Fraser University (in Burnaby, a suburb of Vancouver), and the University of British Columbia (UBC) in Vancouver.

Her first choice was UBC because it had an excellent **education program**, plus Vancouver is an amazing place to live. But, it's also quite difficult to get into UBC because it's **competitive**. You need to get quite high grades in high school to even be considered. After she had sent in her applications, she had to wait for a few months to hear back from the universities.

The first school she heard from was the University of Toronto. She didn't get accepted. She felt disappointed and hoped that she would hear better news from the universities in Vancouver. After a few more weeks, she heard from Simon Fraser. Good news! She got in. And then the next day, she also got good news from UBC.

It was an easy decision. UBC! The other good thing about UBC is that they had a new **student residence** where she could get a private room. It was a beautiful new building and each first-year student could get their own room. This was much better than Simon Fraser University where you had to share a room with a roommate. She replied back to UBC and accepted the offer. She told her friends and family members who were all excited for her. Of course, they would miss her, but they were happy that she got into her first choice.

Vocabulary

graduate: Finish an education program.

community college: Like a university but much smaller. Usually has 1-2 year programs.

trade (job): Trade job examples are a plumber, mechanic, carpenter, etc.

education program: Where people who want to be teachers learn to teach.

competitive: Not easy to win. In this case, not easy to get into a certain university.

student residence: A place where university students live, usually on campus.

Comprehension Questions

1. Why is grade 12 important for Canadians?
2. Do all Canadian students go to university?
3. What is Cindy going to do after high school?
4. Where does Cindy want to go to school?
5. Which schools did she get accepted to?
6. Where is she going to study?

Answers

1. It's important because it's the last year of high school and students have to decide what to do after that.
2. No, there are lots of other options besides university.
3. She's going to go to university.
4. She wants to go to a school in Toronto or Vancouver.
5. She got into Simon Fraser University and UBC.
6. She's going to study at UBC.

Summarize the Story

Using 1-2 sentences, summarize the story. Include only the main details and key events.

Summary:

New Words

Write down any new words that you learned from this story. Consider writing them in a vocabulary notebook or making some flashcards for further review.

-
-
-

Let's Talk More

1. What are common things for people to do in your country after high school? What's the best thing in your opinion?
2. What are some factors that people consider when making this decision?
3. What are some positive and negative things about doing a trade? Would you consider doing a trade?
4. Did you go to university or college? How many places did you apply to?
5. In the future, would you prefer to live in a bigger or a smaller city? Why?

Beginner's Luck

Alex was known for his adventurous spirit and curiosity. One day, while strolling through the streets, he stumbled upon a flyer that caught his attention. It read, "Poker Tournament: Join the thrill of the game and win big!"

Intrigued by the idea, Alex decided to participate in the tournament. He had heard about poker but had never played it before. Determined to try something new, he entered the local casino where the tournament was taking place.

As he entered the room, Alex was amazed by the vibrant atmosphere. The sound of shuffling cards and the excited whispers of players filled the air. He registered for the beginner's table, hoping to meet other novices like himself.

Seated at the table, Alex noticed four other players, all equally nervous and eager to begin. The dealer, a friendly gentleman named Mr. Johnson, introduced the rules and explained the basics of the game.

Each player received two cards facedown. Alex glanced at his cards, feeling a mix of anticipation and uncertainty. He had a pair of fives, and he hoped it was a good hand. He watched as Mr. Johnson placed five cards, known as the **community cards**, face up on the table. These cards could be used by all players to make their best hand.

As the betting rounds began, Alex observed the other players. They seemed focused and strategic, placing their bets with confidence. Alex felt a little overwhelmed and wondered if he had made a mistake by joining the tournament.

However, as the game progressed, he started to gain confidence. He noticed patterns in his opponents' behavior and learned to read their expressions. He also picked up on the strategies they employed. Sometimes, they would **bluff** to deceive others, while other times, they would bet aggressively to scare opponents away.

Alex gradually became more comfortable with the game. He made small bets and carefully observed his opponents' reactions. Surprisingly, luck seemed to be on his side, and he won a few rounds with his modest hands.

The final hand arrived, and Alex found himself with a pair of fives again. Feeling slightly nervous but determined, he decided to **go all-in**, pushing all his **chips** into the center of the table. His opponents exchanged glances, unsure of his move. One by one, they folded, leaving only one player to compete against him.

The tension in the room was palpable as the last community card was revealed. To his amazement, Alex had a full house—a winning hand. The other player hesitated for a moment before reluctantly folding, accepting defeat.

The room erupted in applause as Alex realized he had won the tournament. He was ecstatic, overwhelmed by the thrill of victory. Mr. Johnson congratulated him and handed him a trophy, acknowledging his achievement.

Leaving the casino, Alex couldn't help but reflect on his first poker experience. He had started as a novice but ended up victorious. He had learned that poker was not just about luck but also about skill, observation, and making **calculated decisions**.

Vocabulary

intrigued: Curious about something.

community cards: In the game of poker, the cards that all the players share.

bluff: Lie.

go all-in: Bet all of her or her chips.

chips: Represent money in a game like poker, or other casino games.

calculated decisions: A decision that is deliberate and well-planned.

Comprehension Questions

1. How did Alex know about the tournament?
2. Why did Alex initially feel uncertain about playing?
3. Why did he gain confidence as the tournament went on?
4. Do you think Alex will play poker again?
5. Did Alex win only because he had good luck?

Answers
1. He saw a flyer advertising it.
2. He felt uncertain because he'd never played poker before.
3. He gained confidence because he started to understand the other players' strategies.
4. Yes, probably. It seemed like he enjoyed it.
5. No, it seems like he had some luck, but also some good strategy.

Summarize the Story

Using 1-2 sentences, summarize the story. Include only the main details and key events.

Summary:

New Words

Write down any new words that you learned from this story. Consider writing them in a vocabulary notebook or making some flashcards for further review.

-
-
-

Let's Talk More
1. Have you ever played poker? What was that experience like?
2. Do you enjoy gambling? Why or why not?
3. Why do you think some people get addicted to gambling?
4. Do you think that lottery tickets and other forms of gambling are a tax on poor people?
5. Would you ever go to an event, based on a flyer that you saw like Alex did?

Thanksgiving Dinner

Kim's favorite holiday is Thanksgiving. She loves the food, getting together with family and the changing colours of the leaves. In Canada, Thanksgiving is in October, instead of November like in the USA.

When she was a kid, Kim's grandmother used to cook a big feast that included turkey, ham, **stuffing**, mashed potatoes, sweet potatoes, salads, and pumpkin pie with whipped cream. The adults would have wine, and the kids would have pop. She would eat until she was **stuffed** and then eat a little bit more after that! But her favourite thing was playing with all of her cousins. She'd usually only see them at Thanksgiving, Christmas, and Easter—the biggest holidays in Canada.

When Kim got older, she still enjoyed Thanksgiving with friends and family. Sometimes she'd cook the turkey. It was a big responsibility! You had to take it out of the fridge to **thaw** for a few days. Then, you had to cook it for hours, making sure it was cooked in the middle but not burnt on the outside. There are lots of different ways to season the turkey and everyone has a secret recipe. It isn't easy but everyone said that Kim did a great job with it!

During Covid, Thanksgiving looked a little bit different. Her family members all cooked their own meals at home. The usual things—mashed potatoes with gravy, stuffing, and veggies. Except most people cooked a small chicken instead of turkey. Turkeys are big and are best for at least 10 people. Then, everyone ate together while on a Zoom call. It was a little bit different but still nice to see everyone. They **chatted** for hours and only said goodbye when it started to get late and everyone wanted to clean up all the food and do the dishes. Kim was starting to get sleepy from drinking lots of wine too!

Whether in person or on *Zoom*, one of Kim's favourite **traditions** was for everyone to say what they're thankful for that year. This year, everyone was thankful to be healthy and safe. Others were thankful to have a job and a nice place to live.

Vocabulary

stuffing: Bread with spices, vegetables, butter, etc. that is cooked inside of a turkey.

stuffed: Very full.

thaw: Become not frozen.

chatted: Talked.

traditions: Things that you do every year, usually to celebrate a holiday.

Comprehension Questions

1. Are Canadian and American Thanksgivings on the same day? .
2. What are some foods that people eat at Thanksgiving?
3. Why was Thanksgiving different this year?
4. How much does Kim usually eat at Thanksgiving?
5. Is Kim good at cooking turkey?
6. What is one of Kim's favourite Thanksgiving traditions?

Answers

1. No, they aren't. Canadian Thanksgiving is in October while American Thanksgiving is in November.
2. People eat turkey and gravy, mashed potatoes, ham, stuffing, vegetables, sweet potatoes, and pumpkin pie.
3. It was different because of Covid.
4. She eats a lot until she's stuffed.
5. Yes, she's good at it.
6. One of her favorite traditions is saying what everyone is thankful for.

Summarize the Story

Using 1-2 sentences, summarize the story. Include only the main details and key events.

Summary:

New Words

Write down any new words that you learned from this story. Consider writing them in a vocabulary notebook or making some flashcards for further review.

-
-
-

Let's Talk More

Talk with a friend or classmate about these questions. If you're studying alone, write down 2-3 sentences for each question. There is no correct answer—give your opinion!

1. What's your favorite holiday? Why? How do you celebrate?
2. Have you ever been to a Canadian or American Thanksgiving celebration? How was it?
3. Have you celebrated holidays differently because of Covid-19? How?
4. What are some things that you're thankful for?
5. Does your country have a kind of Thanksgiving/harvest/fall celebration? What is it?

Breaking Up

Emily had been dating her boyfriend, David, for two years, and they had shared many beautiful moments. However, as time went on, Emily started feeling that something was missing in their relationship.

One sunny afternoon, Emily invited David to meet her at their favorite coffee shop. She sat nervously at a corner table, waiting for him to arrive. When he finally walked in, Emily could tell that something was wrong. David looked distant and **preoccupied.**

They ordered their drinks and sat down. Emily took a deep breath and **mustered up** the courage to speak her mind. "David, I think we need to talk," she said softly.

David looked surprised but nodded. "Sure, Emily. What's on your mind?"

Emily took a moment to collect her thoughts. She knew that what she was about to say would hurt them both, but she also knew it was the right thing to do. "David, I've been feeling like we're **growing apart**. We've changed a lot since we first started dating, and I think it's time for us to break up."

David's face fell, and his eyes filled with sadness. "But Emily, I thought we were happy together. Can't we work things out?"

Emily reached across the table and gently held David's hand. "I understand how you feel, David, but I believe this is the best decision for both of us. We've been drifting apart, and it's not fair to either of us to stay in a relationship that doesn't make us truly happy."

David sighed and nodded reluctantly. "I guess you're right, Emily. It's just hard to let go of what we had."

Tears welled up in Emily's eyes as she spoke, her voice filled with emotion. "I know it's difficult, David. We had some wonderful times together, and I will always cherish those memories. But we both deserve to find happiness and fulfillment in our lives, even if it means letting go of what we had."

They sat in silence for a while, absorbing the weight of their decision. It was **a painful moment** for both of them, but they also knew that sometimes letting go was the only way to grow.

Finally, David broke the silence. "Emily, thank you for being honest with me. I appreciate our time together, and I hope we can still be friends."

Emily managed a small smile through her tears. "I would like that, David. It will take time, but I believe we can remain friends and support each other in our journeys."

As they left the coffee shop, their hands no longer **intertwined**, Emily and David knew that their paths would diverge. The breakup was difficult, but it also marked the beginning of new possibilities and opportunities for both of them.

Months passed, and Emily and David slowly rebuilt their lives. They each found new hobbies, made new friends, and discovered a sense of independence. They often ran into each other in town, exchanging friendly smiles and genuine well-wishes. Emily realized that breaking up with David was the right decision.

Vocabulary

preoccupied: Distracted, thinking of something else.

mustered up: Gathered; brought together.

growing apart: Becoming less close.

a painful moment: A short period of time that is difficult.

intertwined: Connected, or linked closely.

Comprehension Questions

1. Why did Emily want to break up?
2. Did David and Emily used to fight a lot?
3. How did David feel about breaking up?
4. Did Emily find it easy to break up with David?
5. Did David and Emily remain friends afterwards?

Answers
1. She felt like something was missing in their relationship.
2. The story doesn't give up information about this, but it seems like they didn't.
3. He didn't want to break up; he thought they could work it out.
4. No, even though it was her decision, it wasn't easy.
5. They are on friendly terms, but it's unclear if they're friends or not.

Summarize the Story

Using 1-2 sentences, summarize the story. Include only the main details and key events.

Summary:

New Words

Write down any new words that you learned from this story. Consider writing them in a vocabulary notebook or making some flashcards for further review.

-
-
-

Let's Talk More
1. Do you think most breakups go as smoothly as the one in this story?
2. Have you ever gone through a painful breakup?
3. What are some things that people do to feel better about life when they break up with someone?
4. What do you think about ghosting someone, if you've only been dating for a few weeks or a few months?
5. Is there a "nice" way to break up with someone?

Christmas in May

Sam was hanging out with his friend Carrie in Burnaby, a suburb of Vancouver. They were at Deer Lake, a popular park. Sam and Carrie were walking around the lake, enjoying a beautiful spring day, when they saw **a bunch** of trucks, equipment, and people. It was quite unusual to see something like that at a public park. "I wonder what this is?" said Sam. "I'm not sure, let's take a closer look," replied Carrie.

So they went to check it out but were soon stopped by a person with a **walkie-talkie**. "You can't come into this area," said the person. Sam and Carrie asked that person what was going on. The person said that they were filming a movie. There are lots of TV shows and movies filmed in Vancouver, so it wasn't so unusual to see this. They asked the person which movie they were filming, and she said that it was a "**made for TV movie**." She also mentioned that it wasn't something they would have heard of.

Sam was still curious about it and wondered if anyone famous was in the movie that he might recognize. He suggested walking around the fence that blocked off access to the set to see if they could get a better look. They walked for a minute or two and then started to see an unusual scene—lots of snow, Christmas lights and other Christmas decorations. The set was a small town designed to look like it was winter, even though May is springtime in Canada. It looked realistic, and they were impressed at how well done it was.

They **peered** through the fence, trying to catch **a glimpse** of the **stars**. But, they could only see lots of cables, crew members, cameras, makeup artists, hair stylists, a snack table and things like that. They couldn't see any actors or actresses. It looked like everyone was setting up because they didn't hear a director yelling things like action or cut. They took a few pictures and continued their walk. It was an interesting experience for them, but they were a little bit disappointed not to see any famous people.

Vocabulary

a bunch = Many; a lot of.

walkie-talkies: Radios that people use to talk to each other.

made for TV movie: A movie that never plays in movie theaters. Instead, it goes directly to TV or online streaming websites.

peered: Looked closely.

a **glimpse:** A brief look at something.

stars: In this situation, refers to actors or actresses.

Comprehension Questions

1. What season is it in May in Canada?
2. Was the snow that they saw real?
3. Did the Christmas scene look real?
4. Did Sam and Carrie see any actors or actresses?
5. Could they go onto the set?
6. What were they disappointed about?

Answers

1. It's spring.
2. No, the snow was fake.
3. Yes, it looked quite realistic.
4. No, they didn't.
5. No, they couldn't. They had to look at it through a fence.
6. They hoped to see some stars.

Summarize the Story

Using 1-2 sentences, summarize the story. Include only the main details and key events.

Summary:

New Words

Write down any new words that you learned from this story. Consider writing them in a vocabulary notebook or making some flashcards for further review.

-
-
-

Let's Talk More

1. Have you ever seen a TV or movie show being made? What did you think?
2. Have you ever met anyone famous? If not, would you like to?
3. Are there any TV shows or movies filmed in your city? Where are they usually filmed?
4. Do you spend a lot of time watching TV shows and movies?
5. How would you feel if a movie was being filmed in your neighborhood? Would you be excited, or annoyed by it?

Ghosted

Like many people his age, Ethan decided to try his luck in the world of online dating. He created an account on a popular dating app, filled out his profile, and eagerly started **swiping right**.

One day, while scrolling through profiles, Ethan stumbled upon a woman named Sarah. She had a warm smile and shared many similar interests. Excitedly, Ethan sent her a thoughtful message, hoping to start a conversation. To his delight, Sarah responded quickly, and they began chatting.

Over the next few weeks, Ethan and Sarah exchanged messages daily. Their conversations were filled with laughter, deep discussions, and shared dreams. Ethan felt a genuine connection growing between them, and he couldn't help but imagine a future together.

One day, as Ethan anxiously waited for a reply to his latest message, something peculiar happened. Hours turned into days, and Sarah's response never arrived. Confused and concerned, Ethan sent a follow-up message, hoping she was okay. But there was no reply.

Days turned into weeks, and Ethan's messages remained unanswered. He couldn't understand what had happened. Had he said something wrong? Did Sarah lose interest? The uncertainty **gnawed** at him, leaving him feeling frustrated and hurt.

Ethan began to question his own worth. He wondered if he was worthy of love and if he had done something to deserve being **ghosted.** His confidence began to **waver**, and he felt the sting of rejection creeping in.

Seeking **solace**, Ethan decided to confide in his close friends about what had transpired. They reminded him that being ghosted was sadly a common occurrence in the online dating world. It wasn't a reflection of his worth but rather a reflection of Sarah's actions.

Slowly, Ethan started to rebuild his self-esteem. He realized that he couldn't control other people's actions, but he could control how he responded to them. He refused to let this experience define his worth or his belief in love.

Months passed, and Ethan continued his journey in online dating. He met new people, had interesting conversations, and even went on a few dates. Although he still thought about Sarah from time to time, he no longer let her ghosting **consume** his thoughts.

One day, while enjoying a cup of coffee at his favorite café, Ethan's phone buzzed. He picked it up and saw a notification from the dating app. Curious, he opened the app and saw a new message from an unfamiliar name.

As he read the message, his heart skipped a beat. It was Sarah. She apologized profusely for her sudden disappearance, explaining that she had faced personal challenges and needed time away from dating. She had thought about Ethan often and regretted how she had handled things.

Ethan sat there, contemplating whether to respond or not. He realized that he had moved on from the pain of being ghosted, and he didn't want to relive those emotions again. He decided to gracefully accept Sarah's apology but kindly declined her invitation to reconnect.

Vocabulary

swiping right: Saying "yes" to someone on a dating app.

gnawed: Caused anxiety over a long period of time.

ghosted: Stopped messaging someone when online dating, without any explanation.

waver: To be unsteady.

solace: Comfort.

consume: Take over completely.

Comprehension Questions

1. How did Ethan and Sarah meet?
2. How was their relationship initially?
3. Why did Sarah ghost him?
4. Did Sarah regret doing this?
5. Why do you think Ethan didn't want to reconnect with Sarah in the end?

Answers

1. They met on an online dating app.
2. It seemed good—they messaged each other a lot.
3. She had some personal challenges. We aren't sure what they are.
4. Yes, Sarah regretted ghosting Ethan.
5. The story doesn't say, but he probably didn't trust her and may have been hurt.

Summarize the Story

Using 1-2 sentences, summarize the story. Include only the main details and key events.

Summary:

New Words

Write down any new words that you learned from this story. Consider writing them in a vocabulary notebook or making some flashcards for further review.

-
-
-

Let's Talk More

1. Do you have any experience with online dating? How did it go?
2. Why do you think someone might ghost another person?
3. If you were in Ethan's shoes, would you have let Sarah back into your life after she ghosted you?
4. How would you have reacted if Sarah ghosted you? Would you handle it as well as Ethan did?
5. Do you think it's better to meet people online, or in real life for romantic relationships?

Halloween

Lauren had recently moved to Toronto from Shanghai for work. One of her coworkers, Sarah asked what she was doing for **Halloween** in a few days. Lauren said that she wasn't doing much and that she honestly didn't even know that much about Halloween. People in China didn't celebrate it, except for some **expats** who would dress up and go out to bars. She'd certainly never done anything to celebrate it.

Sarah had a look of horror on her face! She said that it's the best holiday and her personal favourite because it's just about having fun. She couldn't believe that Lauren had never celebrated it before. Lauren said that she'd probably hand out candy at her house but that she didn't know how many kids would come because it was mostly adults where she lived. She hoped some kids would come so she didn't have to eat all the candy herself! She was trying to cut back on how much junk food she ate!

Sarah, who had two young kids, said that Lauren should come hang out with them and take the kids **trick-or-treating** with her. She told Lauren about the plan. Lauren should come over after work for an early dinner at around 5:30. Dinner was lots of healthy things since the kids would eat so much junk food later. Then, everyone would put on their costumes, get their candy sacks (an old pillowcase) and wait until around 6:30. Sarah's husband would stay home this year to hand out candy. The adults usually bring an alcoholic drink in a travel mug! Then, the kids **rush** from house to house, knocking on doors to get candy!

Lauren said that it sounded fun and that she'd join them. But, she wondered about a costume. Did adults **dress up** too? Sarah said that it was up to her. Maybe 1/3 of the adults who take their kids trick or treating dress up. Lauren said that she'd like to have the full experience so she'd do some research online and find something fun. Sarah mentioned a Halloween store in Toronto, not far from their work that has so many costumes and recommended going there. Now, the only thing left to do was wait for Halloween to come!

Vocabulary

Halloween: A popular holiday in North America on October 31st.

expats (expatriates): People who live in a different country for a period of time, other than the one of their birth.

trick-or-treating: What kids do on Halloween. They go to houses and ask for a treat (candy) or they'll do a trick.

rush: Move quickly; hurry.

dress up: Put on a costume (Halloween or costume party) or wear formal clothes (wedding, etc.).

Comprehension Questions

1. Why didn't Lauren know that much about Halloween?
2. How did Lauren and Sarah know each other?
3. Who is going trick-or-treating?
4. Why does Sarah feed her kid a healthy dinner on Halloween?
5. What did adults often bring trick-or-treating?
6. Where did Sarah recommend getting a costume from?

Answers

1. She didn't know that much because it's not a popular holiday in China.
2. They are coworkers.
3. Sarah, her two kids, and Lauren are going trick-or-treating.
4. She feeds her kids a healthy dinner because they'll eat lots of junk food later.
5. They often bring an alcoholic drink.
6. She recommended that Lauren check out the big Halloween store near their work.

Summarize the Story

Using 1-2 sentences, summarize the story. Include only the main details and key events.

Summary:

New Words

Write down any new words that you learned from this story. Consider writing them in a vocabulary notebook or making some flashcards for further review.

-
-
-

Let's Talk More

1. How do people celebrate Halloween in your country?
2. Have you ever dressed up for Halloween or gone trick-or-treating? How was it?
3. What's your favorite holiday to celebrate? Why?
4. Do you know the history behind Halloween? Look it up on the Internet if you don't.
5. What are some occasions that people wear costumes or get dressed up in your country?

The Lost Wallet

Alex was a **diligent** student, always rushing between classes, part-time jobs, and social gatherings. One sunny afternoon, as he hurried through the crowded streets, disaster struck—Alex realized he had lost his wallet.

Panic set in as he **retraced** his steps, desperately searching for any sign of his missing wallet. He checked his pockets repeatedly, hoping it was just a case of **absentmindedness**. However, his heart sank as he realized the wallet was nowhere to be found.

Feeling helpless, Alex approached a nearby police officer and explained his situation. The officer kindly offered assistance and guided him to the nearest police station. There, Alex filled out a report, providing all the details he could remember about the wallet's contents, including his identification cards, credit cards, and a small amount of cash.

After completing the report, Alex left the police station with a heavy heart. He couldn't help but worry about the inconvenience and financial setback losing his wallet would cause. As he walked dejectedly down the street, he noticed a flyer on a lamppost with the words "Lost Wallet" in bold letters. His eyes widened with hope.

Alex eagerly read the description on the flyer, which matched his wallet perfectly. It instructed the finder to contact the phone number provided. Filled with a **newfound** sense of optimism, Alex quickly dialed the number and explained the situation to the person on the other end.

To his relief, the voice on the phone was warm and sympathetic. It turned out that an honest stranger had found his wallet and was willing to return it. They arranged to meet at a nearby café.

When Alex arrived at the café, he found a **kind-hearted** woman waiting for him. She smiled warmly and handed him his wallet. Alex couldn't contain his gratitude and thanked her profusely. She simply replied, "I know what it feels like to lose something important. I'm glad I could help."

Overwhelmed with gratitude, Alex offered to treat the woman to a cup of coffee. They spent some time chatting and discovered they had shared interests. They decided to exchange contact information.

From that day forward, Alex became more careful with his belongings. He also learned the importance of honest and compassionate individuals like the woman he had met. Losing his wallet had been a stressful experience, but it had also taught him valuable life lessons.

Vocabulary

diligent: Showing care in one's work or other duties.

retraced: Went back over the same route.

absentmindedness: Describes someone who often forgets things.

newfound: Recently discovered.

kind-hearted: Having a gentle nature.

Comprehension Questions

1. Does Alex often lose things?
2. What did Alex first do when he realized his wallet was missing?
3. After Alex went to the police station, did he believe that he would get his wallet back?
4. How did the woman know that it was Alex's wallet?
5. Was there a positive or negative outcome to this story?

Answers
1. No, it seems like losing his wallet was an unusual thing for him.
2. He retraced his steps and checked all his pockets to see if he could find it.
3. It seems like he didn't have much hope for getting it back.
4. The story doesn't say, but she probably asked him what his name was and compared it with the ID in the wallet.
5. It was very positive in the end—he found his wallet and made a new friend.

Summarize the Story

Using 1-2 sentences, summarize the story. Include only the main details and key events.
Summary:

New Words

Write down any new words that you learned from this story. Consider writing them in a vocabulary notebook or making some flashcards for further review.

-
-
-

Let's Talk More
1. Have you ever lost something valuable? What happened?
2. Do you often lose small things in your house like car keys or your phone?
3. Do you think most people would have done the same thing as the woman in this story?
4. What advice would you give to a tourist or international student who lost their wallet in your country? How could they find it again?
5. What kinds of things do you carry in your wallet? What would be the biggest hassle to replace if you lost it?

Going Vegan

Tony was bored one night and was hanging out on his couch, eating potato chips and watching *Netflix*. He was supposed to **work out** with his friend, but he cancelled at the last minute. He was way too lazy to go exercise by himself, so he settled for sitting on the couch. He hated going to the gym alone and would only go if his friend encouraged him.

He didn't have a show that he was watching, so he was just **flipping around** randomly. He thought to himself that he should watch a documentary so that he could learn something! He found one that had an interesting title, "Forks over Knives." He started watching and found it quite good, despite not being the kind of thing that he usually watched. He usually loved watching things like action movies.

The **gist** of it was that eating less meat and animal products and more things like vegetables can make you healthier. You'll have fewer heart attacks and strokes and are also less likely to get cancer. Tony started to feel a little bit uncomfortable and put the potato chips back in the cupboard and got a glass of water. His doctor had recently told him that his **cholesterol** was too high and to start eating more fruits and vegetables and less meat.

He kept watching. By the end, he was convinced that he needed to change his diet and stop eating so much meat. If he kept living like he was now, he thought he'd die early for sure. It wouldn't be easy, but he was convinced that it was important.

Tony got out his computer and did lots of research and found some **vegan** and **plant-based** people on *Instagram* that had some delicious looking recipes. He ordered a couple of vegan cookbooks online: *Oh She Glows* and *Thug Kitchen*. Both of them had excellent reviews. He even looked up some recipes online and made a list of things to buy at the grocery store so that he could start cooking healthier meals. And he even sent a text to his vegan coworker Liz, asking for her help. She was excited for him and said that she'd love to help him out with it. He also decided to try eating vegan for one month and then get his cholesterol checked again to see what the effect was. He guessed that it would be much better.

Vocabulary

work out: Exercise.

flipping around: Using a remote control to scroll through TV or radio channels quickly.

gist: Short summary.

cholesterol: A fatty substance found in the blood and cells. Too much is bad for your health. It generally comes from eating animal products.

vegan: People who don't eat animal products, including things like milk, honey, eggs, etc.

plant-based: Similar to vegan but refers to eating mostly things that grow, as opposed to things that come from animals.

Comprehension Questions

1. Why was Tony sitting on the couch watching *Netflix*?
2. Why did he want to watch a documentary?
3. Why did he choose *Forks Over Knives*?
4. Did he believe what he saw in that documentary?
5. Why did he decide to make a change in his diet?
6. What steps did he take to go more plant-based?

Answers

1. He was sitting on the couch watching *Netflix* because his friend cancelled their plan, and he didn't want to go by himself.
2. He was hoping to learn something.
3. He chose it because he wanted to learn something, and it caught his attention.
4. Yes, he was convinced that he needed to stop eating so many animal products.
5. He decided to make a change because he thought he'd die early if he didn't.
6. He followed some people on *Instagram*, bought some cookbooks, found some recipes, made a shopping list, and texted his vegan coworker.

Summarize the Story

Using 1-2 sentences, summarize the story. Include only the main details and key events.

Summary:

New Words

Write down any new words that you learned from this story. Consider writing them in a vocabulary notebook or making some flashcards for further review.

-
-
-

Let's Talk More

1. Would you ever consider becoming a vegan?
2. Are you a generally healthy or unhealthy eater? Give some examples.
3. Are you becoming more worried about your health, the older you get?
4. Is what we eat the most important factor for our health? Or is something like not smoking or exercising more important?
5. Have you ever watched a movie or TV show that changed your life?

The Hangover

In Vancouver, there lived a young man named Jake. Jake was known for his adventurous spirit and his love for parties. One Saturday night, Jake attended a wild celebration with his friends, where he **indulged** in a little too much alcohol.

The next morning, the sun peeked through Jake's bedroom window, shining brightly on his face. He slowly opened his eyes, only to be greeted by a pounding headache. "Oh no," he groaned, realizing he had a **hangover**.

Jake sluggishly got out of bed and stumbled his way to the kitchen. He desperately needed something to soothe his **throbbing** head. He reached for a glass of water and gulped it down, hoping it would help. However, the relief was only temporary. His head continued to ache, and his stomach felt **queasy**.

As he tried to remember the events of the previous night, he felt a wave of regret wash over him. "Why did I drink so much?" he thought to himself. The room was spinning, and he struggled to keep his balance. Jake's body felt weak and exhausted, as if he had run a marathon.

Feeling miserable, Jake decided to call his friend, Sarah, who had also attended the party. He hoped she would provide some insight into what happened that night. Sarah answered the phone, her voice groggy. She too was suffering from a hangover.

"Hey, Jake," Sarah mumbled. "I'm feeling terrible. Did you have as much to drink as I did?"

Jake admitted his excessive drinking, and Sarah shared a few blurry memories. They both laughed at their foolish **antics** but also regretted their lack of self-control.

Determined to alleviate their hangovers, Jake and Sarah decided to meet at a nearby park. They knew that fresh air and gentle exercise might help them feel better. As they walked through the park, Jake noticed the vibrant colors of the flowers and the pleasant chirping of the birds. The beauty of nature provided a soothing balm to his weary body and mind.

After spending a few hours in the park, Jake and Sarah began to feel more like themselves. Their headaches had subsided, and their energy levels had improved. They realized that having a hangover was a valuable lesson in moderation and responsibility.

The hangover had been a painful experience, but it served as a reminder to make healthier choices. Jake and Sarah embraced a newfound sense of balance in their lives, cherishing the moments they spent with friends while keeping their well-being in mind.

Vocabulary

indulged: Enjoyed.

hangover: What you have the next morning after drinking a lot of alcohol.

throbbing: Pounding.

queasy: Feeling sick to the stomach.

antics: Foolish behavior.

Comprehension Questions

1. Did Jake and Sarah regularly drink too much?
2. Why couldn't Jake remember everything from the night before?
3. Did drinking water help with the hangover?
4. What provided a lasting cure for the hangover?
5. What does Jake want to do in the future?

Answers

1. Yes, it seems like they did.
2. He couldn't remember everything because he drank a lot the night before.
3. Yes, it did, but only for a short while.
4. Jake and Sarah went to the park to get some fresh air and did some gentle exercise to feel better.
5. In the future, he wants to drink less.

Summarize the Story

Using 1-2 sentences, summarize the story. Include only the main details and key events.

Summary:

New Words

Write down any new words that you learned from this story. Consider writing them in a vocabulary notebook or making some flashcards for further review.

-
-
-

Let's Talk More

1. Have you ever drunk too much alcohol? Did you have a hangover?
2. What are some occasions that people drink to excess?
3. What are some good hangover cures, in your opinion?
4. Is going out and drinking lots not worth the hangover the next day?
5. Is drinking and driving a big problem in your country?

Getting a Part-Time Job

Mike was a high-school student in Halifax, Nova Scotia. His parents gave him an **allowance** of $20/week which was more than many of his friends got. However, it wasn't enough to go out with his friends all the time to watch movies or hang out at the mall. Most of his friends have **part-time jobs,** so they had more money than he did. He was a little bit jealous of them being able to buy new clothes or snacks whenever they wanted.

Mike had lots of free time, so he talked to his parents about getting a part-time job. His mom said that as long as he still got A's and B's in his classes, it was fine. She also said that she'd give him a ride to work or he could borrow her car as long as it wasn't too far away from their house. The only problem was that Mike didn't have any work experience. But most of his friends didn't have any work experience either when they got their first jobs.

He talked to his friends at school about their part-time jobs. They gave him some advice like avoiding a certain restaurant where the boss was terrible, or to not do something like **landscaping** because it was too difficult working in the rain or even snow all day.

A few of his friends worked at McDonald's, so he decided to apply there. It would be fun to work with his friends. It wasn't far from his high school so he walked over after school one day, before taking the bus home. He saw a sign outside that said they were hiring. He went inside and asked the person working there for an **application form.** She pointed out where they were on the wall. He grabbed one and sat down in a **booth** to fill it out. It was quite simple and asked for basic information like his name and phone number and took only a few minutes to fill out.

When he was finished, he asked one of the employees if he could talk to a manager. He gave her his application and she mentioned that they needed people right away and asked if he could do an interview then. He said that he had some time so they sat down in a booth and talked for a few minutes. She asked some easy questions about **customer service** and what he would do in certain situations like if someone was complaining about something. The manager thanked him and said she'd give him a call in a day or two. Hopefully he got the job!

Vocabulary

allowance: Money that parents give their children on a weekly or monthly basis.

part-time job: A job that is less than 40 hours/week.

landscaping: Making a yard (or other outside space) more attractive/orderly by cutting the grass, trimming bushes, etc.

application form: What you fill out if you want to get a job.

booth: In a restaurant, a table with benches on either side.

customer service: What employees provide people who buy or use a service at a company. In a fast food restaurant, it involves taking orders and money, serving food, etc.

Comprehension Questions
1. Why did Mike want to get a part-time job?
2. Were his parents supportive of him getting a job?
3. Did most of his friends have jobs?
4. Why did his friends think that landscaping wasn't a great job?
5. Was McDonald's hiring people?
6. Did Mike find it difficult to fill out the application form and do the interview?

Answers
1. He wanted to get a job because he wanted to have more spending money.
2. Yes, as long as he continued to get good grades in school.
3. Yes, they did.
4. They said it wasn't good because you had to work outside in bad weather.
5. Yes, they needed people right away.
6. No, both those things were quite easy.

Summarize the Story

Using 1-2 sentences, summarize the story. Include only the main details and key events.

Summary:

New Words

Write down any new words that you learned from this story. Consider writing them in a vocabulary notebook or making some flashcards for further review.

-
-
-

Let's Talk More

1. Did you get an allowance when you were a kid? How much did you get? What did you have to do for it?
2. Did you have a part-time job in high school or university? What did you do?
3. Do you think high school students should have jobs? Or, should they only study?
4. Is it difficult to get a job in your country if you don't have any work experience?
5. What are some of the first jobs that people have in your country?

Before You Go

If you found this book useful, please leave a review wherever you bought it. It will help other English learners, like yourself find this resource.

Also be sure to check out my other books for English learners, wherever you like to buy books. Just search for "Jackie Bolen" and you'll be able to find them easily.

Made in the USA
Monee, IL
31 January 2024

52725686R00046